THE TRILATERAL COMMISSION:

THE POWER ELITE IN THE FORUM OF INTERNATIONAL
POLITICS and BUSINESS

BY

Myriam M. Gollan

A thesis submitted in partial fulfillment of the requirements for the
degree of Masters of Business Administration
Department of International Relations, Graduate Studies
Canterbury University, UK

January 1996

Word Count: 4396 (Abstract: 118)

Copyright

ABSTRACT

THE TRILATERAL COMMISSION:

THE POWER ELITE IN THE FORUM OF INTERNATIONAL
POLITICS and BUSINESS

The purpose of this thesis is to provide the reader with a general knowledge of the Trilateral Commission by explaining the motive for its foundation, describe the Commission's goals and through a synopsis, familiarize the reader with some of the important members of this organization, and finally what effect the Commission seeks to have on American foreign policy and business affairs.

Initially, it is necessary to supply the reader with an accurate profile of what is conceived today as the elite in American society, in terms of political, social and economic status. By understanding the origins and structures of the power elite, we obtain a clearer portrait of what is representative of a member of the Trilateral Commission.

TABLE OF CONTENTS

TRILATERAL COMMISSION:
THE POWER ELITE IN THE FORUM OF INTERNATIONAL POLITICS AND BUSINESS

LIST OF FIGURES

ACKNOWLEDGMENTS

I would like to take this opportunity to thank my work colleagues at G212. Mr. Joseph Goldman, Esq. for his honest advice and support and Mr. Gary Neuberg, CPO, not only as my department chief, but for his invaluable assistance pointing me in the right direction to find source materials. Back in 1985 both mentors were painfully frank in their effort to dissuade me as to the task. I have made every effort to remain focused on the true intent and hope that posterity will be kind to this minor treatise.

DEDICATION

I dedicate this thesis to my daughter, Tatiana Maria, for whom I pray a better world will be waiting for her to charge into and shape as she grows and learns.

The Author

I. INTRODUCTION

This is the symbol of the Trilateral Commission, a private organization formed in 1973 out of the meetings of the Council on Foreign Relations (CFR). It was the brainchild of David Rockefeller, then Chairman of CFR since 1970.

Figure 1. Trilateral Commission logo

The three arrows symbolize the shared but equal authority of the three superpowers: the United States, Europe and Japan. However, it also represents the balance of power and a forum of shared expertise by its members in three specific categories: the political, the economic and the military. The equilibrium of these three aspects ruled by three of the most powerful nations or continental groups merely reflects the surety with which these leaders view their control or desire to impact developing countries. If the control could not be imposed through suggestions, then at the very least through enticements for progress by encouraging developing nations to espouse or implement programs fostered or conceived by the commission. The nature of these programs could be financial aid in its many forms, or it could be by implementing policies that would inevitably streamline with the CFR's goals together with that state's needs.

Membership was originally limited to 300 members by obtaining the top 100 leaders in their field from each nation. However, those numbers have changed over time. To date there are 490 members. The leaders were recruited and directed by their specific missions and goals were set by the original direction of its founder, David Rockefeller.

Since that time, the Trilateral Commission has gathered the intellectual leaders of their time in order to obtain the best results when addressing problems of great concern for the masses. This paper is an effort to bring to light the many-hued aspects of the commission by studying the variety of expertise in its members, and, reviewing some of its more significant achievements in terms of key placements in government - as a private global organization.

Remember upon the conduct of each depends the fate of all.
Alexander the Great

II. PROFILE OF THE ELITE

a. Origins of Powerful Men

In order to understand the general characteristics and origins of the men in power, we must first realize that the portrait of this particular American species is a collective diagram of all facets of economic, social and lastly, but not the least important, political status.

There are findings as evidenced by C. Wright Mills' studies on the politically elite, that "some 58% of the body of power are from the upper class" (1), meaning five to ten percent of the American population. Of that percentage, most of the politicians were children of politically eminent background if not part of the most socially visible families in the nation. However, historical political eminence did not guarantee inheriting political prowess for most of these men. Instead, their ancestry presented more of a challenge to accomplish any sort of political achievement for the preservation of the family name and prestige. The sole advantage of these men over those with middle and working class backgrounds? Probably the exposure and connections of the upper class to prestigious families, social circles and schools. The comparatively low number of those individuals that did not have to work and study in order to survive the ladder of progress can only be guessed.

Therefore, political ancestry was a good ticket into the circle of this political arena, just as the aristocracy in Ancient Greece took part in and controlled the Senate, yet money and position seemed to have outweighed the reasons for the prevalence of large numbers of upper-class individuals in the sphere of the elite.

Not withstanding, a steady population of the politically elite (approximately 20%) have solid roots from fathers in high-profile or professional careers, self-made businessmen and farmers. (2)

In keeping with this scale of classes then, we can see that the level of college graduates was parallel to the proportion of economic class, the higher the class, the better the chances of college education, and opportunities than those in the middle and working classes.

b. A Sideways Hierarchy

Now that the roots of the elite have been established, it is necessary to place their model inside varying levels of national, federal level and international politics.

Again, here Mills helps us in identifying and collating the powerful structure of the elite into three sectors, those which are: the economic order, the political order and the military order. (3) The first, which is the economic order, where a small group of giant corporations influence, administer and ultimately dominate elements of the economic decision of one or several nations. The political order is characterized by a centralized establishment or organization that permeates and scrutinizes every sphere of the "social structure". Lastly, the military order is self-explanatory. This is the government's "operating" arm, it is the most visible or, when required, the most covert of government bureaucracies and, the most expensive commodity and symbol of power of the American nation, or of any country for that matter.

We must note that none of these orders can become important in and of themselves without the interrelation between the other two, since the process of any foreign or domestic policy must be financially stable, politically sound and militarily supported. Therefore, we should view them as a horizontal hierarchy, fundamentally interconnected and equally invaluable. (4)

III. THE TRILATERAL COMMISSION

a. An Amalgamation of the Power Elite – A World Polity?

We have arrived now at the unification of all three previously mentioned sectors or orders of economic, political and military spheres to describe the ill-famed or controversial Trilateral Commission.

As the International Relations Dictionary defines the organization, the Trilateral Commission is a "private interest group organized to promote understanding and cooperation among Japan, the United States and Western Europe".

Initially the Commission was devised by the Council of Foreign Relations, another private but major body committed to the study of problems of global interest, however, it is one that has attained semi-official status in our government structure. The Council of Foreign Relations (incorporated in New York in 1921) was the American answer to the creation of the League of Nations (formed in 1917). By its formation it rejected subjugation to the British Empire. The Commission was planned for the sole intent of providing decision-making politicians in the international arena with informative papers that could aid in forming opinions and policies in the process of foreign policy.

In 1972, David Rockefeller, president of Chase Manhattan Bank, met in a conference of the Bildenberger society of Belgium (another private sector organization) with several high-level officials to present and discuss the possibility of forming a "little group of opinion makers" or, as Brezinski had previously formulated in his book, "Between Two Ages" 1970, "a high-level consultative council linking Japan, the United States and Western Europe".

From its inception in 1972 to the summer of 1973, when the Commission was formally launched, there was an agreeable reception of supporters. Those included were George McBundy; president of the Ford Foundation, who aided in assigning a sizable amount of the project to the volunteer services of formulating the organization by Zbigniew Brezinski, then at the Institute for International Change at Columbia.

Other members included Henry Owens at the Brookings Institute in Washington, D.C. Therefore, we can safely say that the presentation of this think tank had been closely monitored and perhaps, even silently applauded by some of the most important academics and politicians in this nation. (6)

Therefore, the question arises, is the promoting of understanding between these nations in the interest of American foreign-policy or, is it beneficial to those working towards a "One World Social Order"? The latter premise is posited by Bob White, an anti-Trilateralist and author of the "Duck Book"; a magazine dedicated to the education of the American nation of the impending doom/control that will be brought on by the "one-world-socialist pansy-CFR-Trilateralists'.(7)

b. The Organization's objectives, means and resources.

The commission's main objectives are primarily to provide counsel by specialty members of its organization in areas of finance, sciences, history and politics, to educate leaders and political figures in vast areas of government.

They accomplish part of this informing mission by presenting decisions on specific subjects of vital importance to the membership community.(8) However, the meetings are not made open to the public "to allow more freedom of debate". Though a more apt description of their meetings is "secretive", and seemingly "conspiratorial", this despite the fact that the text of the organization's discussions and presentations are published in their council-funded quarterly: _Foreign Affairs_.

Basically, the Trilateral Commission's stance is one of world mediator and pragmatic problem solver. They posit that threats by political aggressors, anxieties of the Commission's closed-door policies and its political ties to administration leaders do not and will not affect the efficiency or composure of the council's calculations.

Rules of the Commission require that members elected or appointed to an Administration must resign their membership, since it should not appear that the Commission influences the actions and thought process of those policy makers in any respect. Although it is hard to discern when an official has stopped thinking in terms of Trilateralist views and started utilizing his own powers of deduction and resources. Especially when previous to that member's appointment, he may have been exposed to a varying assembly of political and social views as applied to this nation and subsequently the world.

The Trilateral Commission has been accused of being both communist and fascist. It portrays socialist ideals and strains in its supplying of political strategies and supports or postulates ideas of "global information......common scientific language, international peace-keeping forces, home-based education through television and election home-voting consoles, etc....." (9) In total, the Commission is interested in the synthesis of the scientific and spiritual, but without prescribing neither destiny or behavior of mankind. Which, in a manner of speaking, has all the outward characteristics of a socialist oligarchy. The forming of such a group of intellectuals would lead one to believe that their goals and mission do not place an over-abundance of faith in the democratic process of nation states.

In having delineated the social and highly political nature and objectives of this Commission, it is perhaps easier to comprehend why the Commission feels a necessity and commitment to educate leaders of the world powers and "provide measured judgement" for the policy makers. (10)

Perhaps the height of power and influence of the Commission can be seen during the Carter Administration. "Carter was proud of his membership.....he treated it as a kind of graduate seminar in International Affairs", stated Bruce Marlish in his biography of Carter four years later. (11)

Consequently, Carter's appointments to office included fellow members of the organization such as Cyrus Vance as Secretary of State, Zbigniew Brezinski for National Security Council and, Andrew Young, Ambassador to the United Nations, among the most important people. Even though there wasn't exactly the most harmonious of environments with these personalities on the Hill, the anti-Trilateralists were able to show how standard it could become to incorporate a member of the Commission in practically every sphere of government. (One of the most public figures today is Casper Weinberger, Secretary of Defense under Ronald Reagan's administration.)

Presently the Commission has a membership of about 300 comprised from North American, Western Europe and Japan. The North American members include businessmen, university professors, directors of research institutes, congressmen, senators and representatives of the media.

IV. HOPEFUL EFFECTS OF THE COMMISSION ON FOREIGN POLICY-MAKING.

a. Educating Leaders

Although the title seems straightforward, it does not imply that the commission sets out to educate leaders for future roles in government positions. The opposite is quite true. Most, if not all of the members of the commission have at one time or other held positions that increased in responsibility and scope gradually. They moved at an incremental progression from the private sectors of industry, or the corporate world into the federal monetary organizations such as investment and banking, international trade, and finally to serve in government positions in their respective countries. The members of the North American cluster (listed further on) have served as presidents, vice-presidents, secretaries, senators, representatives or even cabinet members in other administrations. (13)

After a close review of the resumes and experience of many of the present and former members, one can see that at particular times during their rise there was an inevitable brush with one of the oldest American educational institutions; Harvard University or, the distinguished London School of Economics in Great Britain. The latter was the institute of "rigeur" for most Latin American aspiring leaders that hoped to return home to make an impact in their country's economics. This was the case with various leaders of South America's Colombia and Argentina.

Almost all members at one time or other sat on the Council on Foreign Relations before they were invited to join the Trilateral Commission. From another perspective, these individuals, having wielded considerable authority in powerful stations before being personally invited by the chairman of the Commission, now choose to move and effect from behind the scenes – as a collective body with a greater vantage point.

The list of members span the various stratospheres of education, science, finance, trade and high level politics. The following is an incomplete list of some of its members but has been created because their names became by-words to the typical American citizen between the 1970's and 1980's and even in present day. They are:

Zbigniew Brezinski, National Security Advisor

Howard Baker and David Abshire in the White House (14)

Richard B. Cheney, Vice President 2001-09 (15)

Henry Alfred Kissinger, US Secretary of State (1973-77) (16)

Walter F. Mondale, Vice President (1977-1981)

Donna Edna Shalala, US Secretary of Health and Human Services (1993) (17)

George Shultz, U.S. Secretary of State, (1969-1970)

Cyrus Roberts Vance, Secretary of State (1977-80)[1] (18)

13. American Hegemony and Trilateral Commission, pg. 166
14. ibid, pg, 171
15. The Trilateral Commission and the New World Order, pg.13
16. ibid, pg.16
17. ibid, pg. 19
18. ibid, pg. 18
19, ibid, pg. 7

David Rockefeller, Chairman of Council on Foreign Relations 1970-1985 (19)

Robert McNamara

Fig.2 Robert McNamara in Cabinet, 1960s

An example of a leader that stood out because of his multi-skilled expertise, erudition, commitment and length of years in the service of the American nation and the international community is Robert McNamara. McNamara's roles set the standard for what a well-rounded leader should resemble. He was president of the World Bank from 1968-1971. Previous to that position he served as U.S. Secretary of Defense from 1961-1968. In 1937, he received his Bachelor's from the University of California at Berkeley and his Master's from Harvard's School of Business in 1939. McNamara entered the United States Army Air Forces in 1943, serving most of his World War II term with duties in the Office of Statistical Control (analyzing bomber's effectiveness). In 1946 he left the service attaining the rank of lieutenant colonel and receiving a Legion of Merit.

After the war, McNamara was hired together with other fellow officers to work for the Ford Motor Company and redirect its business goals. They formed what today is known as the "Whiz Kids". Although that moniker was not given in friendly terms by the Ford workers themselves and, would better describe them more as a gang, these individuals were the first group of young, high-level ex-military officers, now operating in the private business world, to impact their nation by reforming business practices and profits. His ascent into the world of politics and government thereafter is well recorded in history.

McNamara was considered a genius. He was able to successfully handle a wide array of issues ranging from national security, business and economic concerns under the Kennedy administration. During President Truman's presidency in 1963, McNamara created and issued the now famous **Equal Opportunity in the Armed Forces,** Directive 5120.36. This directive dealt mainly with racial and gender equality and concerns within the armed forces.

Although admired and respected, McNamara has been one of few global influencers humane enough to recognize his errors in judgment. This quality is what has set him apart from his piers. Always before him is the failure of the Vietnam war initiative – his Waterloo and his remorse at the costly loss of lives in it.

It would have been extremely predictable to tap McNamara's expertise and mental acumen to then create and foster the progress and growth of the new initiative born in the Council of Foreign

Relations, of which he was a member as the U.S. Secretary of Defense. Today, McNamara focuses his efforts on improving the economic conditions in developing countries by guiding the failing nations through rigorous and tested systems of banking and financial expertise.

Reports Call 3rd World Debt Crisis Severe

By James L. Rowe Jr.
and Caroline Atkinson
Washington Post Staff Writers

Former World Bank President Robert S. McNamara says the cash crisis in the debt-laden developing countries is greater than projected a year ago, but he is more optimistic now that the world's debt problems can be solved.

And in a separate report released today, the Inter-American Development Bank said high unemployment and recession in Latin America could lead to social and political unrest if governments do not try to share more equally the burden of the economic crisis.

The IDB's annual report noted, however, there are strong reasons to expect that the recession-hit nations of Latin America may be able to resume strong growth sometime in the future, although they will likely have to survive with much less cash from overseas.

McNamara, secretary of defense in the Kennedy and Johnson administrations, made his remarks last week at a news conference on a study he co-authored for the Trilateral Commission on economic problems in the developing world. The remarks were embargoed for today to coincide with the formal release of the report, much of which was made available in Rome last April.

The Trilateral Commission is a private group of about 300 business executives, bankers and others from North America, Europe and Japan who meet yearly to discuss common problems of economics and security.

McNamara said there seems to be growing awareness on the part of governments that troubled countries like Mexico and Brazil can solve their debt problems, but that they may need increased economic assistance to give them "more breathing room."

He cited the U.S. Export-Import Bank's decision to grant Brazil $1.5 billion of credits and Mexico $500 million to enable those countries to buy much-needed U.S. products at lower interest rates.

The Ex-Im Bank credits must be approved by Congress. But U.S. legislators generally have been more amenable to granting Ex-Im Bank credits than to voting for increases in the U.S. contribution to official international agencies like the International Monetary Fund and the World Bank. This is mainly because Ex-Im credits finance only U.S. exports and are generally thought to create jobs in the United States.

McNamara and his co-authors—Japanese banker Takeshi Watanabe, founding

Robert S. McNamara

president of the Asian Development Bank, and French economics professor Jacques Lesourne—said in the report that the problem in the debt-ridden developing countries is primarily one of liquidity—temporary shortage of cash—rather than of solvency, the long-term lack of resources to repay debt.

In order to solve liquidity problems, developing countries need more assistance both from banks and from official sources, McNamara said. But countries like Brazil, already in the third year of a deep recession, may need more time to take some of the steps prescribed by the IMF to enable them to end high inflation and reduce the need to borrow, he added.

The steps required by the IMF are the proper ones, McNamara said, and the "only issue is how quickly do you do it and in what amounts." For example, Brazil used to allow wages to grow as quickly as inflation. But under pressure from the IMF, it has agreed to permit wages to grow at only 80 percent of the inflation rate, a painful move that will reduce consumer purchasing power in recession-torn Brazil.

McNamara said there is no doubt that Brazil will be better off when the relationship between inflation and wages is "broken." But it also creates "a lot of pain among low income people," he said.

"If we can't deal with our adjustment [the big federal deficit], how can we expect others to make harder adjustments in a shorter period of time," he said.

Nevertheless, McNamara said, developing countries must take the primary responsibility for solving their economic problems. He said officials in those nations are "far more receptive to accepting that responsibility" than in the past.

The Third World debt crisis has hit Latin American nations particularly hard, because several major countries in the region were heavily dependent on foreign banks for cash to fund development.

In its report, the IDB says that "in the present situation the prospects for external financing are not very promising" and suggests that countries such as Brazil and Mexico will have to rely more in the future on foreign investment capital and official loans from governments and international agencies than they did during the 1970s.

The employment situation in Latin America and its negative impact on income distribution "foreshadow an escalation in social and political tensions," the report said, warning that governments should distribute more equitably "the cost of the adjustment of the economies during the present recession."

About 30 percent of the labor force in Latin America was unemployed or underemployed in the 1981-'82 period, "which means that a growing number of workers are idle or that their already low incomes have been reduced." The report said noted that although unemployment in industrialized nations has also risen in recent years, the jobless in the poorer regions of Latin America are both more numerous and worse off.

The steep recession in the region marks a sharp contrast from rapid rates of growth in the past, the report says.

The Latin American economy, which had grown at real annual rates of 5 and 6 percent for two decades, grew only 1.4 percent in 1981 and declined 1.2 percent last year, the report said. Jorge Ruiz Lara, deputy manager for the 43-nation regional development bank, said in the study that the decline may be even greater for 1983—perhaps 1.5 percent—with possible improvement in 1984.

Latin America's per capita gross domestic product fell 1 percent in 1981 and more than 3 percent in 1982, the report said. "Thus, by the beginning of 1983, the gains made in 1979 and 1980 in raising standards of living had been wiped out."

The report says manufacturing industry has been especially hurt by the world recession and high interest rates of recent years and "is in the midst of what may be the most serious situation to confront it in the 20th century."

After being an engine of growth in the region for decades, manufacturing output "has increased at rates below those of the economy as a whole in six of the last eight years," the IDB said.

Fig. 3   Washington Post, August 22, 1983, 3rd World Debt Crisis

b.   Achievements

The commission's achievements lie not in their collective efforts as a group that has gathered the greatest thinkers in their fields but in the correct placement of their emissaries in the right roles at the precise moment that history requires it. The organization's purpose is to examine and attain solutions to major global concerns. Yet, the commission or the CFR do not operate on the body state as an independent agent. Through the correct mentoring, opening the member's minds to the what other global authorities believe, theorize, exercise and study the problem in question within internal committees, the member becomes well-equipped to meet the challenges set before him or her, in teams, the real political and government arena.

Thus, the Trilateral Commission together with the Council on Foreign Relations have placed the following members in governmental positions to serve the American public through presidential appointments. Three presidents have come from the commission; Jimmy Carter, George Bush and currently Bill Clinton.

Secretaries of State were selected from among the commission and CFR ranks: George Schultz, Cyrus Vance, James Baker, Alexander Haig and Henry Kissinger – all members of the CFR and TC.

Robert McNamara, Harold Brown and Caspar Weinberger served as Secretaries of Defense under Presidents John F. Kennedy, Jimmy Carter and Ronald Reagan, respectively.

On the economic front a few initiatives of import were; 1) Addressing the concerns brought about through the creation of a free dollar standard after President Nixon had eliminated the use of the Bretton Woods system of monetary management and the gold-to-dollar tie in the United States. It's growing opposition by Asia and Western Europe that global monetary policy should not remain in the hands of one nation. 2) The creation of the artificial oil crisis, increased oil prices, reduced production and the management of petro-dollars. Finally, the Commission battled OPEC in the price wars for oil on both American and international soil.

3) The New International Economic Order, was a set of proposals set forth by developing countries in the United Nations Conference on Trade and Development (UNCTAD) in the 1970's. The basic ideology was founded on the French mercantilist ideals that posit that international trade does not yield benefits. The proposal focuses on a central planning economy – meaning allocating resources for planned production from a state or nation. These economic ideas were fostered, presented, and debated at the Council of Foreign Relations – the commission's "parent" organization and became the new byword for developing countries.

CLOSING REMARKS ON · THE COMMISSION

In summation, it is evident that through the analysis of the power elite and an organization thereof, (the Trilateral Commission), one gains a broader perspective of the ingredients that forge economic, political and military circles to influence foreign policies and national interests set forth by a group of high-level academics.

The title of 'academics' is applied to national and international level politicians that temper and monitor the upper classes' weather-vane and promote policies ostensibly beneficial to the masses. These members have all been encouraged and "mentored" to exercise an unusual amount of power in all arenas of social impact whether that implies the private or public office sector. In this sense then, it is with a commitment to integral world harmony and international economic stability that our future administrations should view private organizations (or think tanks) comprised of former political figures, members of giant corporations and figures of military, scientific and technological fields, with a wary eye and a steady hand. It is transparent through time that, as it relates to both these bodies, the CFR and the Trilateral Commission, power has remained in hands of the powerful.

History has shown that the Commission as well as its parent body, the Council on Foreign Relations, is directed and guided by men and women at the top of their game. However, at the helm of this powerful agency sit human beings with beating hearts that in theory are supposed to be looking for ways of improving the quality of lives on a global scale – or are they? We can only hope that the human aspect of the commission's plans and actions and their impact will in time show that their global perspective of bettering the plight of the other three quarters of the world, and their concern for the direction of humankind, guided their minds and their hands to the task.

One should practice caution when embracing the commission's offered policies or theories. It is crucial to remain objective in order to ensure that the power of a nation state remains, if shaky and erratic at best, in the hands of that nation rather than that of a possible universal oligarchy.

Do not let spacious plans for a new world divert your energies from saving what is left of the old.

Winston Churchill

REFERENCES

FOOTNOTES

(1) C. Wright Mills, *"Power, Politics and People"*, (N.Y., Oxford University 1963), p.198

(2) II Ibid II • 'p .200

(3) C. Wright Mills, "Power Elite", (N.Y., Oxford University 1956), p.7 (4) "Ibid".p. 8

(5) Jack Plano, Roy Olton, "International Relations Dictionary", (ABC-CLIO, C a. 1982) p. ·403

(6) Richard Brookhiser, "The Gray /Lurid World of Trilateral Commission", National Review, NOV 81, p .1329

(7) Randall Rothenberg, "The Duck Book", Esquire, OCT 81, p .50

(8) Richard Brookhiser, "'The Gray /Lurid World of Trilateral Commission", National Review, NOV 81, p.1 328

(9) "Ibid". p.1 333

(10) David Rockefeller, "The Trilateral Commission. Explained ", Saturday Evening Post, OC T 80, p.36

(1 1) Richard Brookhiser, 'The Gray/Lurid World of Trilateral Commission ", National Review, NOV 81, p.1 329FOOTNOTES

(12)Richard B r o o k h i s e r ,'The Gray/Lurid World of Trilateral Commission", National Review, NOV 81,p.1329

BIBLIOGRAPHY

Agarwala, P.N., *The New International Economic Order: An Overview*, N.Y., Pergamon Press, 1983.

Domhoff, William G., *"The Powers That Be"*, N.Y., Vintage Books/Random House, 1978.

Domhoff, William G., *"Who Rules America?"*, N.Jersey, Prentice Hall, 1967.

Gill, Stephen, *American Hegemony and the Trilateral Commission*, NY, Cambridge University Press, 1991.

Hart, Jeffrey A., *The New International Economic Order: Conflict and Cooperation in North-South Economic Relations, 1974–77*, London, Macmillan Press, 1983.

Mills, C. Wright, *"The Power Elite" N.Y.*, Oxford University, 1956.

Mills, C. Wright, *"Power, Politics, and People" N.Y.*, Oxford University, 1963.

Sklar, Holly, *Reagan, Trilateralism, and the Neoliberals: Containment and Intervention in the 1980's*, Boston, South End Press, 1986

Sklar, Holly, *Trilateralism: The Trilateral Commission and Elite Planning for World Management*, Boston, South End Press, 1980.

Periodicals

Brookhiser, Richard

"The Gray/Lurid World of the Trilateral Commission" National Review, Nov 1981

Rockefeller, David

"The Trilateral Commission Explained" The Saturday Evening Post, Oct 1980

Rothenberg, Randall

"The Duck Book" Esquire; Oct 1981